# 1,000,000 Books
are available to read at

www.ForgottenBooks.com

Read online
Download PDF
Purchase in print

ISBN 978-0-265-76453-4
PIBN 10971867

This book is a reproduction of an important historical work. Forgotten Books uses state-of-the-art technology to digitally reconstruct the work, preserving the original format whilst repairing imperfections present in the aged copy. In rare cases, an imperfection in the original, such as a blemish or missing page, may be replicated in our edition. We do, however, repair the vast majority of imperfections successfully; any imperfections that remain are intentionally left to preserve the state of such historical works.

Forgotten Books is a registered trademark of FB &c Ltd.
Copyright © 2018 FB &c Ltd.
FB &c Ltd, Dalton House, 60 Windsor Avenue, London, SW19 2RR.
Company number 08720141. Registered in England and Wales.

For support please visit www.forgottenbooks.com

# 1 MONTH OF FREE READING

## at
## www.ForgottenBooks.com

By purchasing this book you are eligible for one month membership to ForgottenBooks.com, giving you unlimited access to our entire collection of over 1,000,000 titles via our web site and mobile apps.

To claim your free month visit:
www.forgottenbooks.com/free971867

\* Offer is valid for 45 days from date of purchase. Terms and conditions apply.

English
Français
Deutsche
Italiano
Español
Português

# www.forgottenbooks.com

**Mythology** Photography **Fiction**
Fishing Christianity **Art** Cooking
Essays Buddhism Freemasonry
Medicine **Biology** Music **Ancient Egypt** Evolution Carpentry Physics
Dance Geology **Mathematics** Fitness
Shakespeare **Folklore** Yoga Marketing
**Confidence** Immortality Biographies
Poetry **Psychology** Witchcraft
Electronics Chemistry History **Law**
Accounting **Philosophy** Anthropology
Alchemy Drama Quantum Mechanics
Atheism Sexual Health **Ancient History**
**Entrepreneurship** Languages Sport
Paleontology Needlework Islam
**Metaphysics** Investment Archaeology
Parenting Statistics Criminology
**Motivational**

CIHM/ICMH
Microfiche
Series.

CIHM/ICMH
Collection de
microfiches.

Canadian Institute for Historical Microreproductions / Institut canadien de microreproductions historiques

## Technical and Bibliographic Notes/Notes techniques et bibliographiques

The Institute has attempted to obtain the best original copy available for filming. Features of this copy which may be bibliographically unique, which may alter any of the images in the reproduction, or which may significantly change the usual method of filming, are checked below.

L'Institut a microfilmé le meilleur ex qu'il lui a été possible de se procure de cet exemplaire qui sont peut-êtr point de vue bibliographique, qui pe une image reproduite, ou qui peuve modification dans la méthode norm sont indiqués ci-dessous.

- [ ] Coloured covers/ Couverture de couleur
- [ ] Covers damaged/ Couverture endommagée
- [ ] Covers restored and/or laminated/ Couverture restaurée et/ou pelliculée
- [ ] Cover title missing/ Le titre de couverture manque
- [ ] Coloured maps/ Cartes géographiques en couleur
- [ ] Coloured ink (i.e. other than blue or black)/ Encre de couleur (i.e. autre que bleue ou noire)
- [ ] Coloured plates and/or illustrations/ Planches et/ou illustrations en couleur
- [ ] Bound with other material/ Relié avec d'autres documents
- [ ] Tight binding may cause shadows or distortion along interior margin/ La reliure serrée peut causer de l'ombre ou de la distorsion le long de la marge intérieure
- [ ] Blank leaves added during restoration may appear within the text. Whenever possible, these have been omitted from filming/ Il se peut que certaines pages blanches ajoutées lors d'une restauration apparaissent dans le texte, mais, lorsque cela était possible, ces pages n'ont pas été filmées.
- [ ] Additional comments:/ Commentaires supplémentaires:

- [ ] Coloured pages/ Pages de couleur
- [ ] Pages damaged/ Pages endommagées
- [ ] Pages restored and/or laminat Pages restaurées et/ou pellicul
- [x] Pages discoloured, stained or f Pages décolorées, tachetées o
- [x] Pages detached/ Pages détachées
- [x] Showthrough/ Transparence
- [ ] Quality of print varies/ Qualité inégale de l'impression
- [ ] Includes supplementary materi Comprend du matériel supplé
- [ ] Only edition available/ Seule édition disponible
- [ ] Pages wholly or partially obsc slips, tissues, etc., have been r ensure the best possible image Les pages totalement ou partie obscurcies par un feuillet d'err etc., ont été filmées à nouveau obtenir la meilleure image pos

This item is filmed at the reduction ratio checked below/
Ce document est filmé au taux de réduction indiqué ci-dessous.

10X   14X   18X   22X   26X
   12X   16X   20X   24X   28X

opy filmed here has been reproduced thanks
a generosity of:

The Nova Scotia
Legislative Library

mages appearing here are the best quality
ble considering the condition and legibility
e original copy and in keeping with the
ng contract specifications.

nal copies in printed paper covers are filmed
ning with the front cover and ending on
st page with a printed or illustrated impres-
or the back cover when appropriate. All
original copies are filmed beginning on the
page with a printed or illustrated impres-
and ending on the last page with a printed
ustrated impression.

ast recorded frame on each microfiche
contain the symbol —► (meaning "CON-
ED"), or the symbol ▽ (meaning "END"),
hever applies.

, plates, charts, etc., may be filmed at
ent reduction ratios. Those too large to be
ly included in one exposure are filmed
ning in the upper left hand corner, left to
and top to bottom, as many frames as
red. The following diagrams illustrate the
od:

L'exemplaire filmé fut reproduit grâce à la
générosité de:

The Nova Scotia
Legislative Library

Les images suivantes ont été reproduites avec le
plus grand soin, compte tenu de la condition et
de la netteté de l'exemplaire filmé, et en
conformité avec les conditions du contrat de
filmage.

Les exemplaires originaux dont la couverture en
papier est imprimée sont filmés en commençant
par le premier plat et en terminant soit par la
dernière page qui comporte une empreinte
d'impression ou d'illustration, soit par le second
plat, selon le cas. Tous les autres exemplaires
originaux sont filmés en commençant par la
première page qui comporte une empreinte
d'impression ou d'illustration et en terminant par
la dernière page qui comporte une telle
empreinte.

Un des symboles suivants apparaîtra sur la
dernière image de chaque microfiche, selon le
cas: le symbole —► signifie "A SUIVRE", le
symbole ▽ signifie "FIN".

Les cartes, planches, tableaux, etc., peuvent être
filmés à des taux de réduction différents.
Lorsque le document est trop grand pour être
reproduit en un seul cliché, il est filmé à partir
de l'angle supérieur gauche, de gauche à droite,
et de haut en bas, en prenant le nombre
d'images nécessaire. Les diagrammes suivants
illustrent la méthode.

| 1 | 2 | 3 |

| 1 |
| 2 |
| 3 |

| 1 | 2 | 3 |

# AN ADDRESS
## TO THE
# PEOPLE OF NOVA SCOTIA.

### INTRODUCTORY.

FELLOW COUNTRYMEN,—

Having for some time past taken an active part in the administration of the public affairs of Nova Scotia, having for the last fifteen years been intimately associated with those who, with the exception of the short period which elapsed between the years 1857 and 1860, administered the Government of this Province, I need not, I trust, offer further apology for this public address. The Hon. Joseph Howe, Provincial Secretary of Nova Scotia, and leader of the present Government, having been honored by Her Majesty with an Imperial appointment, which will necessarily make large demands upon his time, proposes shortly to retire from the administration he has so ably and so wisely conducted. My colleagues holding seats in the Assembly being more or less engaged in visiting their constituencies and organizing where election contests are likely to occur, I have felt that there was a duty owing to the friends and supporters of the Government which, rather than it should remain altogether unfulfilled, I ought, however imperfectly, to endeavour to discharge.

Perhaps I cannot more fitly introduce what I propose to submit, than by taking a retrospective glance of the past, and briefly reviewing the public occurrences of those fifteen years, during which period I have been intimately conversant with public affairs.

### AS MATTERS STOOD IN 1848.

When I entered upon public life in 1848, Hon. Mr. Howe, Hon. Herbert Huntington, Hon. James B. Uniacke, and Hon. Mr. Young, present Chief Justice, were the leading minds giving direction and tone to,—and controlling the public affairs, of Nova Scotia. The great contest of 1847, had just transpired, in which the Liberal party had been triumphantly sustained by the country at a general election.— In a House of fifty-one members, twenty-nine were returned in opposition to Mr. Johnston's Government, and twenty two in favour. On the 22nd day of January, 1848, the new House met, and on the 26th a vote of want of confidence passed by a majority of six. On the 28th day of the same month, Hon. Mr. Uniacke, as Attorney General of the new administration, laid upon the table of the House the two celebrated despatches of Earl Grey, dated respectively the 2nd and 31st March, 1847, conceding to Nova Scotia Responsible Government in all its entirety—but which despatches Mr. Johnston had most disingenuously caused to be withheld for nearly twelve months, and during and until, and after the termination of a general election. From that hour up to the present time, with the exception of the brief period between the years 1857 and 1860, the member for Annapolis has continued to conduct the opposition in the Legislature of Nova Scotia.

At four successive general elections since held, he has been uniformly beaten. We are now on the eve of a fifth general election, and again the Hon. Mr. Johnston has taken the field at the head of the opposition, with a view, if possible, of turning the flanks of the administration.

### RESPONSIBLE GOVERNMENT INTRODUCED.

I shall now briefly revert to some of the more important subjects which have occupied public attention and been disposed of by Legislative action, during this interesting period of our country's history. When Lord Grey conceded the principles of Responsible Government, to use his own expressive language, he but "chalked out a system of administration,"— declaring at the same time and in the same despatch, that "small and poor communities must be content to have their work cheaply, and somewhat roughly done."

It was not until after a fierce struggle even with the principles fully conceded, that responsible Government was practically introduced into Nova Scotia. With sneers and jibes it was laughed at and ridiculed as a time and nicknamed "Responsible Humbug."

At every turn, watching and waiting for any advantage that might offer, with an insidiousness and an untiring determination peculiar to himself, Mr. Johnston inch by inch, step by step, contested the field—never yielding any thing gracefully, never retiring, except for breath, to renew the attack with redoubled fierceness. The first parliamentary conflict I was engaged in arose out of the attempt on the part of the opposition to defeat the enactment of a Departmental Bill. By way of anticipation, Lord Falkland had recently appointed the present Crown Land Commissioner to the office of Provincial Treasurer, vacant by the dismissal of the previous incumbent—and by and with the advice of Mr. Johnston, it was attempted to make it virtually, an office of life tenure, notwithstanding Earl Russel's famous despatch of October 16th, 1839.

## INTRODUCTION OF THE DEPARTMENTAL SYSTEM.

In order to initiate the new system it became necessary to abolish the office of Provincial Treasurer, define and separate the duties, and instead create a Financial Secretary's office for the examination and audit of accounts, and a Receiver General's office to receive and pay out all public money. To accomplish this, occupied well nigh two years of persevering effort upon the part of the Administration. In the House of Assembly, in the Legislative Council, no means were left untried to defeat the policy of the Government, and so get back to the old irresponsible system under which, fogyism flourished, and the voice of the people as expressed through their representatives was but as the wailing of the night winds or the ripple of waves on some lonely sea beach. The Departmental Bill passed both Houses in 1848, and was forthwith forwarded to the Colonial office for Her Majesty's assent. The summer of that year was consumed in correspondence and explanations which ended in the Colonial Secretary eventually deciding, that if the Legislature should, by an address to the Crown, signify a wish that the Act should receive the Royal confirmation, he would submit it accordingly. An address was moved in the House at the next session and may be found at page 211, of the Journals of the House for 1849. There, too, stands recorded side by side an amendment, moved by Mr. Johnston, designed to defeat the measure and crush out the new principle, but which was lost by a majority of seven. Of the twenty-one who voted with him on that celebrated occasion, there was returned at the last General Election but one single man. Six of those, who sustained the Bill, were members of the Assembly just dissolved. I am a little particular in reproducing the records of that day, because the men of that time were thus digging deep and laying stable and firm the foundations of the superstructure which we all so much prize at the present hour.

## ITS EFFECTS.

Had the efforts of Howe and Huntington, of Uniacke and Young, then failed—had Mr. Johnston succeeded in crushing out the nascent principle of Executive responsibility in the germ, of what consequence would it be whether this party or that had a majority in the new House about to be elected? Let this never be forgotten. Men of riper years remember it—they never can forget how ardently, how unwearingly, how faithfully, their representatives then stood up and battled for their rights, for their just influence in moulding the institutions of the country, in thenceforward making and unmaking administrations. It is well that their sons, the young men of the present time, should hear it repeated—should lay it up in their hearts till ere long the pen of the historian records it indelibly in our country's annals.

## SETTLEMENT OF THE CIVIL LIST.

One of the great struggles which, for fifteen long years, agitated and tormented Nova Scotia, was that which arose out of the original reservation of the Crown revenues, and their commutation, for the present Civil List. From 1834 to 1849 this was a vexed question. Long, and wearisome, and angry, were the discussions it produced, but the introduction of Responsible Government, and the sledgehammer arguments and efforts of Huntington and his colleagues, soon put an end to their existence. Referring, lately, to the Journals of the Assembly for 1848, Appendix No. 80, I was rather surprised to find a Minute of the Executive Council of that day, dated 1st of April, 1847, signed, among others, by Mr. Johnston, in which, alluding to the salary of the then Lieutenant Governor, Sir John Harvey, after giving other reasons for its allowance, it is said: "In addition to which, it is obvious that Earl Grey deems £3,500 (stg.) as the more appropriate amount (for the Governor's salary), and it is not more than His Excellency's experience, and that of his predecessors, indicate *as necessary to meet the expenses of the high station.*" And yet so lately as the 22nd of March, 1862, *fifteen years subsequently*, when our population has increased fully one-third, and our revenues *more than doubled*—in 1862, Mr. Johnston and his political friends, with a view to clap-trap popularity, undertook to reduce the salary of the Lieutenant-Governor to £2,500, sterling. (See the Journals of 1862, page 61.) What a comment is here upon consistency! In 1847 Mr. Johnston and his friends were *in office*—in 1862 they were *in opposition!*

### IMPORTANT LAWS BEGIN TO BE ENACTED.

Passing to other subjects, permit me to remind you, gentlemen, that the act to render the Judges of the Supreme Court independent of the Crown, and to provide for their removal in certain cases—an act regulating the appointment of Sheriffs, thus remodelling, improving, and settling our institutions on a firm basis, were passed shortly after the date of the advent of the old Liberal progressive party to power.

### RESULTS.

Cribbed, cabined and confined as the popular branch of the Legislature had heretofore been under a regime adapted only to the state of an infant community—a regime that swathed the intellect of the country in its contracted cerements, waged fierce conflict with every nobler attribute of our nature, that attracted no popular notice to the possessor unless "to the manor born." now that it was discovered that "the well understood wishes of the people, as expressed through a majority of their representatives," was henceforth to dictate, an influential position in the Assembly began to count for something. But just in the same proportion it concentrated upon the heads of prominent leading men, the opposition, and animadversion of those whose prejudices it encountered, whose positions it unsettled, and whose power it undermined. Hence the antagonism of the leaders of the Opposition of that and the present day, to the men whom the majority of the people delight to honor. Hence his unrelenting opposition to their services, and all who sustain their policy up to the present hour.

### MR. JOHNSTON'S MISTAKES.

Once at least, perhaps twice, in his history, Mr. Johnston might have honorably retired from the arena of political strife. His vindictive temper probably outran his judgment, and for himself, the more the pity. No great measure has ever found its way upon our Statute book, no public improvements or provincial work, from the days I refer to, up to the present hour, have been suggested, enacted or matured by his political opponents, that have not received his fiercest opposition. To-day he stands almost alone, as the representative survivor of these scenes—the embodiment of the narrow, unexpansive policy which was then overthrown, and the ghost of which, I suspect, will never be exactly laid, while he has personal and denominational friends to any extent, whom he can rally, or upon whom he can rely.

### OUR PUBLIC WORKS.

When those great public works which, by and bye are destined to be, not merely an index of the foresight of the ablest minds among us—I mean our railways—when ere long they will be counted among the most judicious investments of public money ever disbursed, as well for the promotion of peaceful, agricultural and mercantile pursuits, as for military and defensive purposes,—when these were projected and advocated by a portion of the same class of men who had secured for us and all posterity, Constitutional Government, there was he at the head of his forlorn hope, resisting, protracting, misrepresenting, and as far as in his power lay, defeating and counteracting their efforts. But the great resistless tide of public opinion rolled on, nevertheless, the old landmarks were washed out, and the opposition phalanx began to be thin and shattered. Men of mark, who, side by side, had fought his first campaigns and felt that there was no longer reason nor room for further resistance, refused to again to enlist in such hopeless, fruitless struggles. Their country had better use for their talents, and cheerfully placing themselves at her disposal, one after another their services have been accepted.

### POLICY REVERSED.

When Mr. Johnston found that his antiquated notions and fossil ideas of governing a young, rising Province like Nova Scotia, were no longer viewed with favor by any class, he then performed one of the most extraordinary political somersets ever witnessed. He commenced to strike out an opposite extreme. From being the advocate of a despotic, irresponsible policy, at one wild leap, all of a sudden, he rushed into rampant republicanism. He now became the advocate of elective Legislative Councils, and with his own hands laid the foundation of the universal suffrage franchise. This act, as may be seen, originated in the report of a committee of the House of Assembly, dated 3rd April, 1852, of which *Mr. Johnston was chairman*. Mr. Doyle's act, based upon payment of rates, had not given satisfaction, and a committee, at the head of which stands the name of the member for Annapolis, referring to Doyle's Bill, reported as follows: "They recommend in lieu of that franchise, that the House should substitute a franchise based on *universal suffrage*, qualified by residence." See Journals of Assembly, 1852, App. No. 87,—and in the same year he brought forward his Elective Legislative Council Bill, which was defeated. This Bill was kept prominently before the House and country up to the 6th day of March, 1856, when a division, taken upon the subject, was had, and will be found recorded, page 84 of the Journals for that year. In 1857 he obtained office with a large majority in both Houses, when he could easily have carried it, had he ever been sincere. It was finally abandoned in 1858, sent out to the country for "an airing," with the Prohibition Liquor Bill—neither of them ever found their way back—and the cry for an Elective Legislative Council has never since been renewed in Nova Scotia. What a career for a public man to exhibit!

### THE CHANGE OF GOVERNMENT IN 1857, AND THE CAUSE.

In the speech from the throne for the year 1856, the present Chief Justice being leader of the Government, a clause was inserted, promising "a measure for the improvement of general education." A Bill based upon taxation for common schools was introduced accordingly, obtained a second reading, and the principle of assessment adopted, by a majority of 28—37 for the Bill, 9 only against. Mr. Johnston, Dr. Tupper, and their political supporters voted for it. See Journals 1856, page 112. And here dates the origin of the difficulty which terminated early in the session of 1857 by a hostile vote which overthrew the Government, defeated all educational legislation up to the present hour, and drew the line of party division very nearly, where it has ever since remained.

The Roman Catholic members in the House, and the denomination as a body throughout the country, raised an objection to the measure, and refused to sustain it, unless the Government would consent to engraft upon it, a clause entitling them to "Separate Schools." Without the aid of the members of that body, and others who represented constituencies which they could influence, the Government, otherwise numerically the strongest that Nova Scotia had ever possessed, could not carry this measure. It had, therefore, to be abandoned for the session. Difficulties broke out upon the line of Railway works which required to be dealt with firmly and vigorously, and an antagonism having arisen between the present leader of the Government, and a section of persons of this denomination, with the leading men of whom he had been associated for a quarter of century, eventually ended in an open rupture. The enemy ever alert to improve such an occasion to divide and weaken a party that had become all powerful in the country and in the Legislature, industriously fanned the flames of rising discord. Not that Mr. Johnston hated the Roman Catholics less, nor loved Mr. Howe more, but with the eye of a keen and practised politician, he saw that the time had now arrived, which, if rightly improved, might restore him to power and possibly, nay *probably* secure him the prize at which he had been aiming for the last quarter of a century. He had himself originated the only religious war cry ever raised within the Province. He had for twenty years previously been denouncing the Catholics as a dangerous class of people, and they had as zealously denounced him as the enemy of their religion. Never man had more effectually defied and alienated a class of Christians than he had—could he now—how could he, stoop to receive them to his confidence, beckon them to his councils, and affect to forget the past, when every body knows he never forgets an injury, nor forgives an affront? How could he trample under foot all the professions of his past life, and accept office at the hands, and as the gift of a class of persons in his heart of hearts, he neither loved, honored, nor respected—persons with whose teachers and leaders he had been at open hostility for the whole period of his political life? But he could, and as the sequel proves he did. The prize glittered as he gazed upon it. The ermine was attractive. The temptation was irresistible. At the commencement of the Session of 1857, Mr. Johnston was prepared to make the sacrifice. It was great, he did not underestimate the cost, but yet the prospect. It was the temptation to which in "No Name" Magdalen yielded under the manipulation of Captain Eragge when she consented to marry Noel Vanstone, only with an unhappier sequel. He formed his Government early in 1857, and a more subservient pliant majority than he had at command, to do his bidding, never did homage to leader or master. Looksly's bugle horn in "Ivanhoe" summoned his retainers not more certainly to his aid than did Mr Johnston's whistle call his majority ever to his back during these three years. It was a sad day for Nova Scotia, when this unnatural alliance took place. Extremes met. Nine members elected to sustain the existing administration walked across the floors of the House, and were now fast friends of the new Government.

### THE EFFECT UPON THE TREASURY.

The public works, as a matter of course, the unfinished Railways, and the management of them, fell into new hands, and were subjected to their control. Mr. Forman, the Chief Engineer, was obnoxious to his superiors, and must make way for a more pliant, less scrupulous officer. Such an one was speedily found in the person of a Mr. Laurie, of whom and of whose qualifications the world had never before heard, and of whom, so soon as he had served the turn required, it knows as little. His salary of $6000 a year—more than that of any two of the puisne Judges of the Supreme Court, nearly equal to the pay of the Attorney General, the Receiver General, and the Financial Secretary added together—was ominous of the way the public money was to be spent, now that after ten long years the old Opposition leader had vaulted into his new place. It is a painful recital, but it must be repeated nevertheless. In round numbers, the entire amount of contracts let for constructing our 92 miles of Railway, was £416,029 9s. 4d. For this the parties who contracted to do the work were bound to complete it, and the Gov-

ernment had ample security to compel them. But it is scarcely credible, and yet it is true, that no less an amount than £121,621 19s. 6d. additional, in shape of extras, was paid, before these works were taken off the contractors' hands! It is usual, in heavy works of this kind, in making estimates, to leave a margin of ten per cent. to cover all extras, but here was an excess of nearly thirty per cent.! Of this large sum for extras, but £10,881 18s. 11d. were paid before the Government changed hands, and the enormous sum of £100,487 8s. 3d. was paid out during Mr. Johnston's short administration—paid out of the Railway fund to rapacious contractors, many of whom, like Laurie, came, nobody knew whence, and have gone, nobody knows where. I have never said, nor do I now say, that no part of this immense sum of money was rightfully due; but I have said in my place in the Legislature, and I repeat it here, nobody knows it better than I do—I am familiar with the proofs—they are under my hand—I repeat it—the facts are as I now give them. What would have been a fair and proper allowance to have made the contractors I am not prepared to say; but this I do say before the people of Nova Scotia, and I shall ever contend for it, the amount allowed was exorbitant, outrageous, and entirely indefensible. I affirmed so much upon the hustings at the last election at Truro. I published it in the presence of William Henry and John J. Marsh , both members of the Administration that had made such havoc with our Provincial funds, and neither of them ventured a denial. I repeated it a few days ago in my place in the Legislative Council, in the presence of the late Receiver General, the Hon. Stayley Brown, who paid over this vast sum. I characterized it then, as I do now. I held under my hand the proofs, as I hold them now. I threw down the guage, and no man has hitherto dared in my presence to accept it. It has given mortal offence to my political opponents, as the people of Nova Scotia are aware.—But why? Not because the statement was unsubstantiated, but simply because it was *true*; and the books in the Railway Office contain the written records showing when, where, how, by whom and to whom all the money was paid. In the Journals of the Assembly for 1861, Appendix 51, tabulated details of what I now refer to are all elaborated, a copy of which I subjoin prepared, not by me, nor under my direction, but at a time when I was confined to my bed, unconscious of what was going on in or out of the Legislature, in consequence of injuries received upon the Railway in the discharge of my duties in the winter of that year.

Before passing away from the subject of the extras, I make one further observation. How comes it to pass that if I had made an unsubstantiated statement on the hustings at Truro, why is it that that statement has from that hour up to the present, so troubled, irritated, annoyed and worried Mr. Johnston and Dr. Tupper. A hustings oration never before excited so much attention. What nomination speech in the whole history of this country was ever previously considered of sufficient importance to deserve the uninterrupted attention of the press for three long years—to be criticised, denounced and controverted in Parliament at every successive session during the existence of an entire Assembly? Why or wherefor all this anxiety to counteract the effect of a statement if it were unfounded and indefensible? Gentlemen, electors of Nova Scotia, like the blood on Bluebeard's key, neither Mr. Johnston nor Dr. Tupper can wipe the stain away. It is simply because the statements I have made on this subject are true, that they command so much attention and I am honored with so much and such undeserved notice on their part. They are *true*—the books and vouchers in the Railway office prove that they are *true*. Messrs. Johnston and Tupper know they are *true*, and a vast majority of the public believe them to be *true*.

A MISAPPROPRIATION OF RAILWAY FUNDS.

But the above, I regret to say, was not all, nor the worst part of Railway mismanagement, by a great deal. For although having access to the books, papers, and vouchers in the Railway Office, I had ascertained the state of matters there, I did not then know what I have since ascertained, and now vouch under my own signature as derived from the books kept in the Receiver General's office, and other public documents, that a further sum of over £100,000, interest included, was abstracted from the Railway fund by the financial officers, Hon. Mr. Stayley Brown and J. J. Marshall, Esq., and applied to defray the current expenses of the Government during those three years they held office. In 1857, their expenditures having exceeded their revenue, they improperly took out of the Railway fund £1,733 17s., to make ends meet. In 1858 they repeated the operation, only growing bolder, they ventured to take out and misappropriate the further sum of £15,894 10s. 5d. In 1859, their last year, going backwards, as they were doing, at a fearful ratio as will be seen, growing familiar with such peculation, they actually misappropriated of Railway money, obtained by sales of Debentures and otherwise, the enormous sum of £79,310 7s. 2d., in all amounting to £96,933 14s. 7d.! (For proof see the speech of Hon. Mr. Anderson, delivered in the Legislative Council, page 73 of the Debates of 1861.) But not a word or syllable of all this was allowed to escape the lips of a single member of the Administration. Mr. Johnston, Attorney General, as leader; M. I. Wilkins, for a portion of the time, and Mr. Henry for the remainder, Solicitor Generals; Dr. Tupper, Provincial Secretary; Stayley Brown, Receiver General; John J. Marshall, Financial Secretary; John Campbell, Charles Campbell, and John McKinnon, members of the Government, some, or all of them were the depositors of this grand state secret, and it was well kept. But it transpired at last. The vigilant, scrutinizing eye of the present Receiver General soon after he took office, discovered the fraud and exposed it. In presence of the Hon. Stayley Brown, in his place in Parliament, it was by Mr Anderson charged upon him and the late Government. No defence was attempted: they were dumb. They could neither defend nor deny it. So late as the present Session, in my place in Parliament, I again charged it upon the Hon. Mr. Brown, late Receiver General, but he essayed no reply, defence, or explanation. Nothing, I fearlessly affirm, in all the past history of this country is to be compared to this high-handed, unauthorized, concealed, misappropriation of such a vast amount of the public money of the country.

### THE PICTOU RAILWAY.

As a political party, these very individuals and their friends—the men who did this unhallowed deed—are now canvassing the County of Pictou, modestly asking the suffrages of the electors, to enable them again to get control of the finances of the Province—again to manipulate its revenues—again to take such unwarranted liberties with the public funds. Yes, the funds that should have been disbursed in extending our lines of railway—money, had it been well and wisely expended, sufficient to have constructed nearly one-half the branch to Pictou, is now irrecoverably gone, and they who spent it—have their candidates in the field at Pictou and elsewhere, asking to be honored with your confidence. Every man of their party in the Assembly, leader and follower, Jas. McDonald *alone excepted*—and he looked well nigh frightened out of his life as he sat among the Government supporters, for the first time in his public career—voted against the bill to construct the first section of eleven miles of the Branch Line! A Railway to Pictou, as the condition of political support, is in the mouth of every man you meet from that fine flourishing county, and yet, strange to say, the party who unlawfully spent the money set apart to build it, who have uniformly opposed it, who now oppose it with all the money, influence and means they can bring to bear, oppose it as a party, oppose it all but unanimously, have the conscience and the modesty, at this time of day, to ask the electors of Pictou to vote against the very candidates upon whom the Government rely for aid to enable them to complete the undertaking *now happily commenced.*

### THE LIBERALS IN OPPOSITION AND MR. JOHNSTON IN POWER.

The liberal progressive party had long discharged the functions devolving upon them in power as a Government. Their position was now reversed. They were honored to conduct the opposition, a much less onerous, and a much less responsible duty. How they discharged these functions, I need not tarry to recount. The only really unsettled question of a public character which existed when they resigned office, was a long pending dispute with the Mining Association, relative to the terms of an outstanding lease improvidently granted to the Duke of York, held by his creditors and assignees. The difficulties connected with the settlement of the matter, which had run over a long period of years, were all but overcome, and on the point of being finally arranged, when the Government changed hands, and the finishing stroke, the winding up of a tedious and intricate negotiation thus accidentally fell under the control of the late Government. The present Attorney General, who had largely contributed to promote the solution of the difficulties, and had taken an active part in moulding public opinion on this side the water, was selected to aid the leader of the Government of the day, in finally and amicably adjusting the matter with the company's agents in London. The policy and the terms of the settlement, as everybody knows, were substantially the acts of Mr. Young's administration. Mr Johnston, during the whole period of his political career, or nearly so, had been the retained counsel of the Association, sitting in Parliament and using all his influence there to protect their interests. His own political supporters had at last refused to sustain him in his action longer, and so making a virtue of necessity for once in his life, he consented to co-operate with his political opponents, and terminate this difficulty. Dr. Tupper and the Hon. R. B. Dickey have on one or two occasions been setting up claims to credit on the part of Mr. Johnston's administration for promoting a settlement of this dispute. He himself has never claimed credit in the matter so far as I know. There are too many resolutions and amendments recorded on the Journals of the Legislature to admit of that, and he and they have just about as much right to credit in this case as the fly had, that perching himself on the end of the coach axletree when the driver plied his whip and the wheels whirled rapidly forward, flapped his little wings, and cried out "see what I have done." Just about.

This is about the only matter of any moment, which excusably characterized Mr. Johnston's Government during the three years they held office. Dr. Tupper claimed that a delegation on which he served, commissioned to promote the construction of the Intercolonial Railway, had given it "a valuable impulse." But how, or in what way, he never explained,—and nobody up to this hour has ever been able to discover. His recent conduct, and that of his colleagues, in opposing the only feasible scheme that has ever commended itself to a majority of the members of the Legislatures of the Provinces of Nova Bootia and New Brunswick are the ablest comment afforded of the kind of advocacy on his part of this great measure. He and his associates in the House of Assembly, McFarlane and Donkin, they three and the tw Legislative Councillors, Messrs. Pineo and Dickey, of Cumberland, the only county in the Province, Halifax excepted, that has two resident Legislative Councillors, they have now proved themselves uncompromising enemies and opponents of this great work.

THE DISSOLUTION AND GENERAL ELECTION OF 1859.

Eventually the period for a dissolution of the Assembly arrived. With a firm tread and a confident attitude, strong in the purity and integrity of their principles, although greatly weakened numerically, trusting and confiding, nevertheless, in the soundness of the policy they had ever advocated, the old liberal progressive party made their appeal to the country. Their opponents then, as now, affected to despise them. They said they were "like drowning men catching at straws." Dr. Tupper had declared he would "rout them horse, foot and artillery, and send them cowering to the wall." But the gallant yeomanry of the country, the men

"Who kept the bridge so well,
In the brave days of old"—

who had sustained Howe and Huntingdon in the trying time, when majorities in the Assembly counted for nothing,—now that they counted for everything, were not to be daunted, they were not going to desert their principles nor forsake their friends in the hour of extremity. Never at any general election for the previous twelve years, had the country mistaken the issue, or wavered in its integrity, and the returns of the 12th May, 1859, as they came in from the several counties, townships, and districts, proved that threats had not frightened, sophistry had not mislead, nor could money purchase the suffrages of a majority of the independent, intelligent electors of Nova Bootia. In a House of fifty-five members on the first division, there were but twenty-five found to sustain the Government, whilst twenty-nine were opposed. A mean, though dexterous piece of manipulation on the part of Sheriff Kerr, of Cumberland, unseated Mr.

Fulton, who had the majority of votes for that county, and returned Mr. McFarlane in his place, or the majority in the House would have been 31 to 24. A change of Government ensued as a matter of course, but never did politicians part with power so reluctantly, as did this condemned administration. I will not weary the reader by enlarging here. It is all too recent, and too fresh in our memories, to need recital. I will, therefore, now shortly call attention, briefly, to the state of public affairs as the old Government left and the new Government found them.

FIRST OF THE CONDITION OF THE RAILWAY.

It was allotted to the writer, as is well known, take charge of the Railway Department. I accepted at the same time the office of Solicitor General, the duties of which I have ever since discharged gratuitously. The salary of this office is £100 stg. per annum, which in four years, amounts to $2000. That sum small, some may say, nevertheless, is raving the first, secured by this arrangement. On assuming office I found a Chief Commissioner of Railways and two assistants, receiving $4,400 annually for managing the road. This I considered totally unnecessary. The two assistants having resigned, I declined to recommend successors, and a saving was thereby affected of $1,600 per annum. I found Mr. Mosse at a salary of $2000 per annum; but as the work of construction had ceased, I had no occasion for the services of a Civil Engineer, and I dispensed with him. I found that for the year 1859 the entire earnings of the road were not enough to pay its working expenses by upwards of $8,000. What the opponents of Railways had prophesied, namely, that when finished they would forever be a burden upon the Provincial Revenue, I found they were taking good care should be literally fulfilled. We had thus already got the first instalment of the p        deficiency.

The road receipts earned         $102,877
And the working expenses were    111,276
                                 _____
Showing a deficiency of            $8,399
for 1859.

I immediately proceeded to reorganize the whole concern, and in nine months from the 1st April 1860, ending on the 31st December, of the same year, the road had not only paid all its working expenses but a surplus of $20,270 into Treasury. For the year 1861, after paying all expenses, there was a net balance of $26,802.78 clear profit, and for the year 1862, of $37,181.48. Mark the progress. Thus under the changed administration the difference has gone on increasing so, that comparing my last year 1862 with theirs of 1859, we have the round sum of $37,181.48 added to $8399, making in all $45,580.48 as representing the difference—the difference between a road managed one year under one Government, and the same road managed another year under another.

But be it borne in mind, that under the former government, Mr. McNab's salary, as well as the salaries of Mr. Scott and Mr. Shannon were *not paid out of* the earnings of the road, but out of the construction fund, the money borrowed to *build it*. Had they been paid *out of the earnings*, as I have since paid salaries, instead of the deficiency of 1859, being as it was $8,399.00, it would have been $4,400.00 more — in all, $12,799.00. In four years, this would have amounted to $49,696.00. Take neither the highest nor the lowest of the years of my administration—as an average, take the year 1861, and the road earned over and above working expenses, $26,802.00; multiply this by four years, and we have $107,208.00 as four year's earnings. Four years of deficiencies such as 1859 would, as shown, be $49,696. These two sums, therefore, added together, represent as real gain to the country, in one department of the public service, secured by the change of Government, a sum equal to $156,804. These are calculations easily understood, based on data entirely reliable, and incapable of being controverted. I accordingly subscribe my name to them, and hold myself prepared to substantiate them, at all times and in all places.

It has been matter of surprise to some persons how Mr. Laurie could have increased the extras as he did. Let me explain on two items only. When the contracts were let, rock cuttings were tendered *for* and taken to be excavated at an average, say, of a dollar a yard, measured in *situ*—that is, in the solid rock—and till he came here, contractors were paid accordingly, and nobody had ever dreamed of any other [principle. What did *he* do? Why, he said a yard of solid rock, if broken up, would make a *yard and a half*,—and so, instead of a dollar, he allowed fifty per cent. additional. In No. 5 section he added 11,165 yards ; in No. 3 he added 13,355 yards ; No. 4, Windsor Branch, 28,926 yards—(see App. No. 1, Journals 1860). Here, at $1 per yard, are extras of $78,561.

The earth was calculated by the yard at, say thirty or thirty-five cents a yard, and the contracts let by the measurement before it was dug. But he measured the *fills* not the *cuts*, and as earth shrinks after it is once dug, he allowed 8 per cent. for what he called shrinkage. This was another and a bright idea to line the contractors' pockets at the expense of the Province.

If a man agreed to sink a shaft 3 feet by 8, 99 feet deep, you would call that 33 yards of rock, cubic measure. Not so Laurie. He adds 16½ more, measuring not the hole, but the pile of broken stone. To get money out of the Province, when they had to cut through earth and fill up a hollow, then he reversed the principle, and as earth shrunk while rock swelled, he charged Nova Scotia per per cent. on a single contract, No. 8 Main Line, 10,000 yards, very nearly. This, thus plainly put, will interest some people, I know.

But it has been alleged that I reduced the salaries of some of the officers, discharged others, and abolished offices. I did. But I never discharged a man whose services were required, and I never reduced a salary so low, but that I have ten applicants for every vacancy. My only difficulty has been, to know how, when vacancies occur, to choose capable officers without offending others equally competent. But then it was also alleged that while I reduced the salaries of others, I did not reduce my own. I reduced the annual expense of superintending the department $800. So far as the first two years of my administration is concerned, it is quite true that I received the salary of my predecessor. But when the Provincial revenues of 1861 fell off, in consequence of the American difficulties, although the Railway revenues did not suffer, but largely increased, I stepped forward nevertheless, and did what no public man of the Opposition was ever known to do—I voluntarily relinquished $400 per annum of my own salary, and ever since, for $2,400, I have discharged the duties that Mr. McNab, Mr. Shannon, Mr. Scott, Mr. Morse, and Mr. Wm. Henry, as Solicitor General, discharged, and for which they received at the rate of $69,000 per annum, saving the Province the difference of $46,000 annually! Let the country, therefore, now fairly understand the true position of matters connected with the Railway administration. Such is the contrast offered by a comparison of things as they are in 1863, and as they were in 1859. But for the difficulties with which I have had to contend, arising out of the hostility of political opponents, my success in the administration of the Railway Department would probably have been still more triumphant. But as the public know full well, everything that malice could invent, and tortured ingenuity devise, has been done, with a view of embarrassing me and counteracting my efforts to economise the public revenues and ensure a safe and successful administration of the department over which I have presided. It has been the chief point of attack for the whole three years, and every enemy of progression, every opponent of the Administration, has seemed to feel that he had a special duty to discharge in heaping abuse, misrepresentation, and obloquy upon it. The public were admonished, cautioned, warned, forbidden at the risk of their lives, to trust themselves in the cars; yet, in spite of all that could be done, said, or written, the road and its management have steadily won their way to public confidence. Upwards of 300,000 people have now passed over the lines since I have had charge of their management, and under Providence, not an accident—no, not one—has happened to a single passenger on the trains during all that time.

### THE OLD AND THE NEW ENGINE HOUSES.

Mr. Laurie, among other things, left me as a legacy, an uncouth unfinished structure, intended for an Engine Shed, looking not unlike the ruins of a Chinese Joss house. Completed, it would hold but eleven engines—we had twenty—without a roof, the walls unfinished, it had cost the Province over $10,000. Competent architects condemned it, as incapable of supporting the roof intended for it, and having been left exposed a whole winter, to repair damage would cost $1,600, to have finished it $13,300, exclusive of ventilating the site. It had to be taken down, therefore, and another erected. A new one, capable of holding twenty engines, costing but $10,163, was erected in place of it, and there it stands to-day one of the most complete and perfect structures of its size in America—an ornament to the grounds, and a credit to the contractor.

### RETRENCHMENT IN OTHER DEPARTMENTS AND FIRST OF THE ASYLUM FOR THE INSANE.

When the change of Government occurred, this Institution, as is well known, was found to be in a wretched condition. It, too, had to be reorganized. The Medical Superintendent, the Secretary, and the Board of Management, were all in open discord. The pruning knife was vigorously applied—the Commissioners dismissed and the management entrusted to the Board of Works. The savings resulting from this operation have averaged nearly $9,500 yearly—and in four years will effect a saving of, say $38,000.

### SALARIES AND LEGISLATIVE EXPENSES.

Messrs. Johnston and Tupper held the Government for three years, and upon careful comparison I find that the expenses of the Legislature and for salaries during the next succeeding three years were less by upwards of $14,000 than they were during the three of their administration, and but for the tiresome repetitions and repeated constitutional debates each session, forced on and kept up for days and sometimes a week at a time by the Opposition leaders, these savings would have been very much greater than they are.

### THE MEASURES OF THE ADMINISTRATION.

I observe that the Opposition Press has lately been asking what has the present Government done and what has the administration to show for the three years they have held office. A good deal, I reply—a good deal, considering the destructive policy continually adopted by their opponents.

In the Session of 1860, an important Act was passed, "Introducing the system of decimal currency," a system simple, and easy to reckon by, to which the public are now becoming accustomed, and one which will soon supplant the old method of counting by pounds, shillings and pence.

A Bill passed the same Session "to provide for the organisation of a Volunteer force for the defence of the Province." This was another valuable measure—the handy work of the present Government. The system of the initiation of money votes by the Executive Government as in England and the sister Colonies, was also a valuable measure and well adapted to protect the public interests by abolishing what was known as the "log rolling" practice. This too was the work of this first session. An important alteration was made in the Laws regulating the mode of taking of a Census, and during the vacation that followed a Commission consisting of the Attorney and Solicitor General and the Financial Secretary, with Stephen Fulton, Esq., acting as their Secretary, compiled one of the most valuable, reliable, and important sets of statistical tables, to be found in any of the British Colonies. The original manuscript returns, all bound up, constituting a most interesting record, are deposited in the Legislative Library in Halifax, accessible to every body in all time coming.

### THE VACATION AND THE PRINCE'S VISIT.

In the summer of 1860, despite all the efforts, both of Mr. Johnston and Dr. Tupper, to mar and prevent, the Government succeeded in procuring for His Royal Highness the Prince of Wales a right hearty, and most enthusiastic reception in Nova Scotia. Attempts to disturb the harmony so much to be desired on such a festive and joyous occasion, ebullitions of ill concealed jealousy and spleen, all went for nothing. As the time approached when the Prince was about to land upon our shores,—overwhelmed with confusion and shame, they could not stand entirely aloof, but their factious, frozen hearts were never fairly thawed out or gladdened all the while the Prince was in the Province. They were more anxious,—much—to have interviews with the Duke of Newcastle, present political memorials, and bore him with their grievances than to afford a joyous welcome to the Prince. The Colonial Secretary declined to entertain their complaints, and they have never forgiven him for it—and never will.

Dr. Tupper shortly after undertook to ignore the status and functions of the Colonial Secretary by passing him over and pouring his complaints into the ears of Earl Russel, the Foreign Secretary of State, but he got ignored himself, his communication was treated with contempt, and he was taught a lesson he is not likely to forget for the remainder of his political life. During the same year the Government set on foot negotiations in regard to the Intercolonial Railway, which have eventually terminated in the Provinces of Nova Scotia and New Brunswick, passing an Act identical in all its details, adapted to consummate this long discussed and long projected measure. But of that more fully hereafter.

## DISCOVERY OF GOLD.

The discovery of gold in Nova Scotia occurred in the year 1861, and imposed upon the Government a delicate and difficult duty, one for which no previous training had qualified any of the public men of the country. In some localities gold was discovered on ungranted lands, in others on lands granted, but in which the right to all the mines and minerals was reserved to the Crown. How to make these available without doing injustice or injury to the owners and possessors of the soil, was the grand difficulty, to solve which, neither California, Australia, or Columbia could afford a ray of light, or so much as a hint to guide. A gold bill, however, after great labour, care, and study bestowed upon it, was prepared and submitted to the Legislature shortly after its opening in 1862. The extent of gold bearing rock, or of alluvial deposits, was at that time little understood, and the bill was framed upon such information as then existed. Throughout the summer of 1861, the only mode of managing the gold mines, was by orders of Council, prepared under an Act which had previously passed, adapted to regulate not gold mines, but coal mines. As new discoveries were made, these orders required to be altered and modified from time to time, and when the Legislature met a bill was submitted. It passed, slightly amended, into a law. New discoveries and further developments have since necessitated further modifications, but most of the leading features of the Act of 1862, the rental clause excepted, are still retained, and are found incapable of being improved. The principle of a rental, provided by the Act of 1862, has now been abolished, the gold fields are thrown open to enterprise and speculation in the most unrestricted manner. A royalty sufficient merely to cover the expenses of a vigilant superintendance and administration of the Department is imposed, and the legislation at present provided, is evidently giving great satisfaction.

The Gold Act, and another for the Incorporation and winding up of Joint Stock Companies, in addition to the ordinary legislation, were the leading valuable measures passed in the session of 1862. In addition to these the Administration revised, remodelled, improved and recast the whole militia law of the country. This measure, although it has attracted but little notice or remark hitherto, was a most important and valuable labor. Under the vigilant eye of His Excellency the Commander-in-Chief, the Volunteer and Militia forces of this Province are quietly assuming an organization and attaining an efficiency which at no previous period of the history of the Province ever characterized them. The process is necessarily slow; effective drill is not learned in a day; but if we should be seriously threatened with difficulties on our frontiers, as these provinces may at any unexpected moment be, then the value of such organizations, previously provided, would be properly appreciated. But, as in everything else, not only the Gold Bill, but the comparatively small amount required to re-organize the militia, did not escape the active, hostile opposition of those who, right or wrong, must needs oppose every act of the Government.

## FINANCE.

The session of 1862, owing to the derangements which the American revolution produced in the financial affairs of all the Provinces, was one adapted to put to the strongest proof the capacity of the Executive Government, and to test the manliness, integrity and firmness of their supporters. A great and unexpected falling off had occurred in the revenue, owing to the civil war, which had broken out just as the session of 1861 had closed. When the session of 1862 opened, although the credit of the province had been sustained intact, yet a public debt of upwards of $120,000 had accumulated, to provide for, and pay off which, without disarranging the institutions of the Province, was well adapted to task the energies of men of the best minds of any country. The ministry and their friends affirmed that the embarrassments had arisen out of the civil war, and from causes beyond their control, and, as trade found new channels, would speedily pass away. This the Opposition denied. They asserted that it arose from the incapacity of the government, who should have foreseen if not obviated the war. They alleged that there was no remedy for it now, but a reconstruction of the whole financial policy of the Province. The emergency was so vast, so alarming, according to the views of the Opposition, that faith must not only not be kept with the public officers all over the province, but the whole Civil List settlement must be broken up, public pledges violated with Her Majesty, and a new state of affairs inaugurated. But the men upon whom the responsibility of the Government rested, took a very different view of the matter. They proposed that a slight additional duty of 2½ per cent ad valorem be imposed, some specific duties be raised a trifle, new duties placed upon home-brewed ale and home-manufactured tobacco, and in three years, at the furthest, the debt would be paid off. Dr. Tupper then moved his grand retrenchment scheme, which was voted down. The Government policy was adopted; and, instead of three years, within nine months the whole debt was paid off—a handsome surplus remaining in the treasury—and the increased ad valorem duties act repealed again within a twelve month. The Opposition leaders were sincere, or they were not. If sincere, they evinced their utter incapacity to deal with such questions. If insincere, then their untrustworthiness and treachery are not the characteristics which should commend them to the confidence of the people of Nova Scotia. In either aspect of the case, therefore, they prove themselves deficient of the qualities indispensable to the characters of statesmen, or farseeing financiers. At the beginning of 1863, the whole debt of the previous year was paid off—the ad valorem duties reduced down again to 10 per cent, the lowest tariff in America—the public service suitably provided for—and a grant of no less than $140,000 given for the roads and bridges for the current year. Here, then, is a complete and triumphant refutation of all the malevolent accusations and charges of all the opponents of the administration already urged, or which the fertile inventions of their friends may prefer, during the political campaign in which the country is now engaged, —a refutation, complete and triumphant.

### THE LAST SESSION.

And now for the session of 1863. Again I am proud to be able to point to further important measures of great public utility, and well adapted to promote the best interests of the country. By the skill, energy and ability of the administration, the necessary legislation for constructing the great intercolonial line of railway is at last recorded upon the Statute book of the country. A scheme designed, in concert with Canada and New Brunswick, matured so far as the maritime Provinces are concerned, has been perfected in Nova Scotia by the untiring efforts of the great progressive party. Notwithstanding the untruthful announcement in the opposition press, Canada has begun to move in the matter, and a sum amounting to $10,000 has been inserted in the Estimates for the present year for proceeding with a survey. (See the Quebec *Mercury*, Government organ, of the 29th April.)* A

* Since the foregoing was written, the Canadian Government has been defeated, one of the grounds being their faithlessness towards Nova Scotia and New Brunswick in reference to the Intercolonial Railway.

first section of a Branch line to Pictou to tap her great coal fields, to bring the remotest portions of Cape Breton within twenty-four hours of Halifax, is provided for by law and already in course of construction. Against both these measures, every opponent of the present Administration, in the House of Assembly, leader and follower,—James McDonald only excepted—*voted dead*. Even the Cumberland members, with Dr. Tupper at their head, I grieve and am ashamed to have it said,—they of all others, offered every opposition in their power to both these acts. By rail, the remotest residents in Cumberland, dwelling on the frontiers of New Brunswick, if the Intercolonial succeeds, could reach Halifax easily in six hours, (and St. John in the same time) avoiding the snows of the Cumberland mountains, the fatigues of a two or three and sometimes a six day's journey. By it farmers would enjoy easy and ready access to the two best markets in the Provinces, and a choice of either—and yet they, the people of Cumberland, have sent to the Legislature men who have thus dared to misrepresent them, and their best and dearest interests, regardless of all consequences. Well so be it. Their accountability is in the right place. If Cumberland expected this of her members, it is all as it should be. If not, if her best interests have been trifled with and sacrificed, her expectations disappointed, and her pride wounded, she has it now in her power to administer a well deserved rebuke.

Then we have also an Immigration Bill passed this last Session adapted to invite labor and capital and enterprize into the country. Its fruits are already beginning to be felt. Mechanics, laborers, and household servants, of a superior class, are flowing quietly but steadily in the desired direction. A Bill to stimulate the farmers, and to improve the condition of our Agriculture, has been enacted. Large premiums are offered for the best stock, the best productions of the farm, and to encourage emulation and rivalry among the stock-breeders in all parts of the Province. These are results of exertions made by the Government, and those who support them in the Legislature. The Act to raise the Franchise, after the ensuing election, has become the law of the land. It is safe upon the Statute Book also, and notwithstanding all that may be said to the contrary, commends itself, I feel assured, to the sound judgment and enlists in its favor, the dearest sympathies of a vast majority of the sincerest well-wishers of our common country.

### CONCLUSION.

And now in conclusion, a word or two as to the coming contest. The period which the law provides for the termination of Parliament has arrived, and power for the next four years must be exercised according to the "well understood wishes of the people as expressed through a majority of their representatives." Candidates who favor the policy of the present Government, and make their appeal accordingly, occupy a platform such as it is rarely the good fortune of a political party to possess. The public treasury is in a healthy and satisfactory condition. Trade flourishes on every side. The Coal measures of Cape Breton and the Eastern Counties are pouring forth their rich produce and furnishing freight more or less remunerating to our shipping. The quartz rocks of Halifax, Guysboro', and Hants are producing rich returns for the labour bestowed in developing their secret deposits. The ring of the shipwrights axe and the caulkers mallet is heard in the creeks, on the shores, and along the inlets of every County in the Province. The farmer sees prospects of fair prices for his produce, and a ready market for all he can raise. Real penury or pinching want is almost unheard of among us; activity prevails on all sides, and Great Britain has not a Province among all her wide possessions, in more prosperous circumstances this day, than Nova Scotia. If so, where the necessity for change? What is the country to gain by revolutionizing its affairs under circumstances like these? What may it not lose?

That is a question easier asked than answered. Judging from the experience of the past—looking at the rapid accumulation of debt contracted during the three short years the present Opposition held power, with nothing to show for it—and bearing in mind the unscrupulousness with which they misappropriated money borrowed for other purposes, and without which they would have retired from office with the Province over $400,000 in debt—the accumulation of but three years, —with such facts before us, one cannot but feel that there are grave reasons why it is not desirable that the same class of persons should, for light or unimportant reasons, be permitted again to have the control of our public affairs.

I have now discharged a duty, which I felt that some member of the Administration owed to the country. For reasons already assigned, I have assumed the responsibility of the task. I only regret that continuous calls and unceasing demands upon my time, disable me from discharging this duty more satisfactorily. That I shall attract some further unenviable notoriety by this address, is far from improbable. It matters little, any way. My opponents must have already well nigh exhausted their quivers of every poisoned shaft. All that has been said or written about me for the last four years, has but nerved me for the position I occupy. Better men have, perhaps, been better abused, that alone ought to afford some consolation.

With confidence in the judgment, the discretion, the energy, and the vigor of the old liberal progressive party of Nova Scotia, I look forward, gentlemen, hopefully and cheerfully, to the decision which this country will on the 28th day of this present month pronounce upon the issue submitted,—and in the meantime, remain, Your obdt. servant,
J. McCULLY.

*Brunswick Place,*
*Halifax, 8th May, 1868.*

## NOVA SCOTIA RAILWAY.

*Statement showing "the amount paid to each Contractor on the Railroad according to agreement—the amount paid to each for Extras—under whose Government—and on what authority."—In reply to an application of Hon. A. F. Comeau.*

| No. of Contract. | Contractors. | Amount of Contract. £ s. d. | Amount of Cont'ct work executed. £ s. d. | Gross amount of Extras. £ s. d. | Extras paid by Mr. Forman. Under Mr. Young's Government. £ s. d. | Under Mr. Johnston's Government. £ s. d. | Total. £ s. d. | Extras aris'g from re-measurement by Mr. Laurie, paid under Mr. Johnston's Gov't. £ s. d. | Extras paid by Mr. Poole, under Mr. Howe's Government. £ s. d. |
|---|---|---|---|---|---|---|---|---|---|
| M. Line. | | | | | | | | | |
| 1 | Cameron & Co............ | 22925 0 0 | 22694 0 0 | | | | | | |
| 2 | Black & McDonald...... | 9398 0 0 | 8998 8 0 | | | | | | |
| 3 | { Creelman & Co.......... Wm. Turnbull............ | 24201 0 0 | 21062 8 0 291 7 0 | 29 4 3 788 5 8 | 29 4 3 | | 29 4 3 475 13 0 | 1835 2 1 | |
| | Johnston & Blackie...... | | 2641 0 0 | | 475 13 0 | | | 312 12 8 | |
| 4 | Black, McDonald & Irons. | 46360 19 8 | 46177 8 1 | 8946 15 1 | 672 18 3 | 8940 14 9 | 4613 13 0 | 4333 2 1 | |
| 5 | Donald Fraser............ | 16798 8 6 | 16798 3 6 | 1987 4 0 | 1225 7 0 | 219 13 0 | 1445 0 0 | 542 4 0 | |
| 6 | Sutherland & Sons........ | 30774 10 11 | 30774 10 11 | 22625 15 1 | 1794 10 0 | 5150 19 3 | 6945 9 3 | 16680 5 10 | |
| 7 | Johnston & Blackie...... | 41616 18 4 | 40425 0 6 | 10722 17 1 | 1415 1 10 | 3289 0 10 | 4704 2 8 | 6048 14 5 | |
| 8 | Sutherland & Sons........ | 21993 8 10 | 21889 0 3 | 4073 1 10 | | | | 4073 1 10 | |
| 10 | Sutherland & Sons........ | 31696 19 7 | 30228 9 8 | 2307 11 3 | | | | 2307 11 8 | |
| 11 | { Walker & Co............ Donald Fraser............ | 19879 5 8 | 18716 3 0 | 5314 10 5 5589 18 2 | | | | 5314 10 5 5589 18 2 | |
| W. Branch. | | | | | | | | | |
| 1 | { Cameron & Co.......... Johnston & Blackie...... | 33305 0 8 | 14554 0 0 17841 10 2 | 7811 17 10 | 105 0 10 | 3355 9 8 | 3460 10 6 | 4351 7 4 | |
| 2 | Duncan McDonald........ | 28000 0 0 | 27336 7 0 | 9478 7 7 | 199 14 4 | 5883 9 6 | 6083 8 10 | 3395 3 9 | |
| 3 | { Cameron & Co.......... Johnston & Blackie...... | 41411 11 5 | 14067 0 0 26552 14 3 | 25555 19 5 | 754 10 9 | 7705 7 4 | 8459 18 1 | 17096 1 4 | |
| 4 | Cameron & Co............ | 47458 13 0 | 47028 19 3 | 6585 2 1 | 1226 0 8 | 2928 4 1 | 4154 4 9 | 1178 0 0 | 1252 17 4 |
| 5 | Duncan McDonald........ | 21500 0 0 | 21822 17 6 | 7866 1 2 | 2983 18 0 | 2139 2 9 | 5123 0 9 | 2232 5 4 | |
| Extension. | do. | 8709 18 4 | 8709 18 4 | 585 1 7 | | 83 18 9 | 83 18 9 | 501 2 10 | |
| | | 446029 9 4 | 437498 8 8 | 121621 19 6 | 10881 18 11 | 34695 19 11 | 45577 16 10 | 74791 8 4 | 1252 17 4 |